Searchlight BOOKS™

How Does Energy Work?

Investigating Light

Sally M. Walker

Lerner Publications Company
Minneapolis

Lerner Publications Company
A division of Lerner Publishing Group, Inc.
241 First Avenue North
Minneapolis, MN 55401 U.S.A.

Website address: www.lernerbooks.com

Library of Congress Cataloging-in-Publication Data

Walker, Sally M.
        Investigating Light / by Sally M. Walker.
            p.   cm. — (Searchlight books™—How does energy work?)
        Includes index.
        ISBN 978–0–7613–5774–2 (lib. bdg. : alk. paper)
        1. Light—Juvenile literature. I. Title.
    QC360.W3464 2012
    535—dc22   2010029952

Manufactured in the United States of America
1 – DP – 7/15/11

Contents

Chapter 1

WHAT IS LIGHT?

Have you ever tried to run away from your shadow? Have you ever made faces in front of a mirror? Without light, you couldn't play these games.

Playing games with light can be fun. But we also need light. Why is light important?

Light is a form of energy. Light lets us see the world around us. Light also makes heat. The sun gives off a lot of light and heat.

Sunlight

Light from the sun makes life on Earth possible. Sunlight carries energy to plants and animals. Sunlight also carries heat to Earth. All water on our planet would freeze without the warmth from sunlight.

Most of our light energy comes from the sun.

Other Light Sources

Fire makes light and heat too. A fire can be used to heat things or to make an area bright. Light energy from lightbulbs brightens buildings and neighborhoods. Some lasers use light energy to cut things.

The red light on this remote controls the television.

Atoms and Photons

Light is very important. But where does it come from? Light comes from tiny particles called atoms. Atoms are so small that billions of them would fit on the period at the end of this sentence.

Like you, atoms can get excited. An atom becomes excited when it gets extra energy. The particles inside an excited atom move faster. If the atom is excited enough, a small burst of light energy shoots out. This small burst of light energy is called a photon.

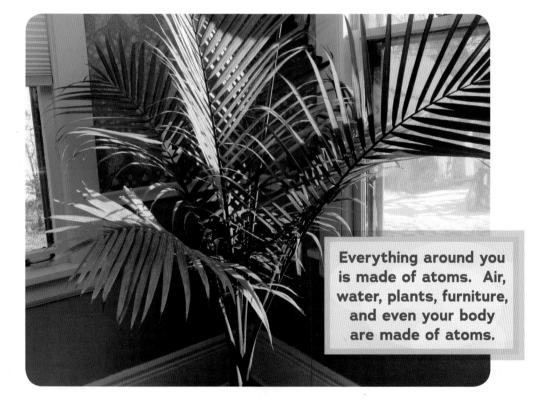

Everything around you is made of atoms. Air, water, plants, furniture, and even your body are made of atoms.

A photon streaks out from a light source. Excited atoms on the sun shoot out photons all the time. The photons travel in rays. Rays are narrow beams of light. A laser's ray is a moving stream of photons. So are the rays of light from a flashlight.

Light rays move away from their source in all directions at once. That's why the light from one lightbulb can make an entire room brighter.

lightbulb

light rays

Light rays move away from a light source in all directions.

8

Chapter 2

MATTER AND LIGHT

Everything around you is made of tiny atoms that have joined together. When two or more atoms join together, they make a molecule. A molecule is bigger than an atom. But it's still very small.

These kids are pretending to be atoms that are joined together. What do we call two or more atoms that have joined together?

The rock is solid. The milk in the cup is liquid. What kind of matter is the cup?

Atoms + Molecules = Matter

Atoms and molecules make up matter. Matter is anything that can be weighed and takes up space.

Some matter is solid, like rocks and furniture. Some is liquid, like milk or water. Matter can also be a gas. The air we breathe is made up of gases. So what does matter have to do with light?

Usually we can't see light rays moving. But we can sometimes see light rays when they hit matter. You can make light rays visible. How?

Experiment Time!

YOU WILL NEED ALUMINUM FOIL, A FLASHLIGHT, A PIN, A SPOONFUL OF FLOUR, AND A SHEET OF NEWSPAPER.

Spread the newspaper on the floor close to a wall. Cover the light-making end of your flashlight with aluminum foil. Use the pin to make a tiny hole in the center of the foil. Fill the spoon with flour, and set it down on the newspaper.

Usually the light from a flashlight spreads out as it travels. But the light will travel as a narrow beam through a pinhole.

Turn off the light in the room. Turn on the flashlight. Point it at the wall above the place where you put the newspaper. Can you see a spot of light on the wall?

AROUND THE ME

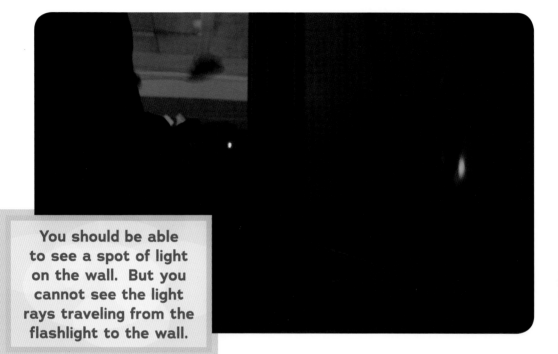

You should be able to see a spot of light on the wall. But you cannot see the light rays traveling from the flashlight to the wall.

Pick up the spoonful of flour. Gently blow the flour toward the space between the flashlight and the spot of light. Can you see the light beam? Yes. The flashlight's rays travel in a straight line to the wall. You can see the rays now because they are hitting the flour, which is matter!

Chapter 3

LIGHT BOUNCES

We can see objects because light rays reflect off matter. *Reflect* means "to bounce off." Light rays reflect off objects the same way a ball bounces off the ground. If an object reflects no light rays, we cannot see it.

Light keeps traveling until it hits something. Then it bounces like a ball. What happens when light bounces off an object?

Prove It to Yourself

Go into a room with a wall mirror. Bring a flashlight with you.

Make the room as dark as you can. If it is totally dark, you won't see the walls at all. That's because no light rays are reflecting off the walls. If you can see the walls dimly, some light is in the room. It is reflecting off the walls to your eyes.

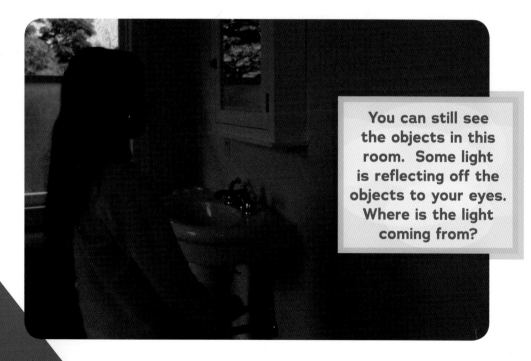

You can still see the objects in this room. Some light is reflecting off the objects to your eyes. Where is the light coming from?

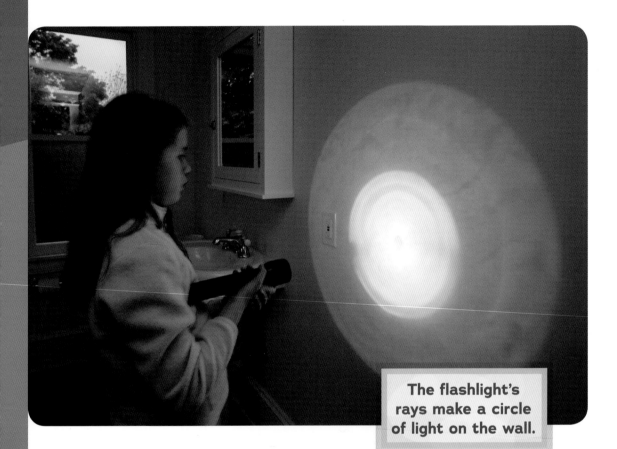

The flashlight's rays make a circle of light on the wall.

Hold the flashlight in front of your chest. Turn it on and point it straight at an empty wall. The wall absorbs many of the light rays. Other rays are reflected back to your eyes. How do you know?

You know because you can see a circle of light where the rays reflect off the wall. The part of the wall that is not reflecting light stays dark.

Look down at your shirt. Is there a circle of light on it? No. Not enough rays are reflected to make a circle of light on your shirt.

The wall is rough. So the light rays that hit it bounce off in many different directions. Only some of the rays are reflected back to you.

Now Try This!

Stand in front of a mirror. Hold the flashlight chest high again. This time, shine the light straight at the mirror. Look down at your shirt. Is there a circle of light? Yes. Why?

The circle is there because the mirror reflects more light than the wall does. The mirror's surface is very smooth. Smooth surfaces reflect a lot of light. Most of the light rays striking the mirror are reflected back onto you.

The mirror reflects enough light to make a circle of light on your shirt.

Chapter 4

LIGHT BENDS

Light shines easily through eyeglasses. What kind of matter are eyeglasses made of?

Some light rays are not reflected. Instead, they pass through certain kinds of matter. Matter that light can pass through very easily is called transparent. Air is transparent. So are water and clear glass. Light rays shine easily through these materials.

Other Kinds of Matter

Some matter lets only a few light rays shine through. That dims the light. Matter that some light can shine through is called translucent. Wax paper, milk, and thin cloth are translucent. Fog and wispy clouds are translucent too.

Clouds are translucent when a little bit of sunlight shines through them.

Some matter stops light rays completely. No light shines through them at all. This kind of matter is opaque. Bricks are opaque. So are aluminum foil and a thick block of wood. Your body is opaque. That's why you cast a shadow. A shadow is an area where light rays could not pass through.

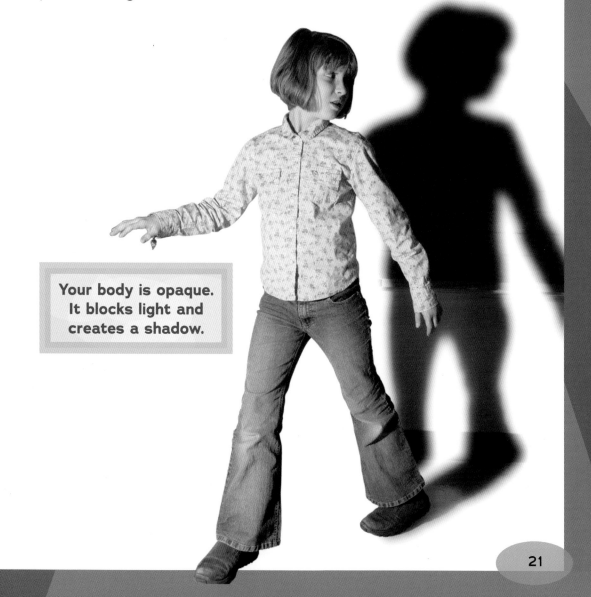

Your body is opaque. It blocks light and creates a shadow.

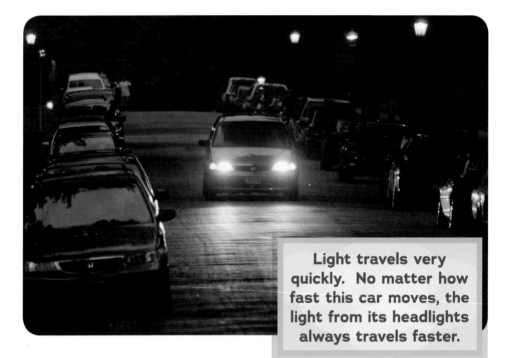

Light travels very quickly. No matter how fast this car moves, the light from its headlights always travels faster.

Light Moves Fast

Light rays travel very quickly. They travel much faster than you can blink your eyes. Light rays in outer space race at a speed of 186,282 miles (299,792 kilometers) per second. Light rays slow down when they enter Earth's air. Even so, a light ray from the sun takes only eight minutes to reach Earth. A rocket would take many years to make the same trip.

Light rays can bend when they pass from one kind of matter into another. They bend because their speed changes. The bending of light rays is called refraction. You can see light rays refract. You will need half a glass of water and a pencil or a pen.

YOU CAN USE THESE OBJECTS TO EXPERIMENT WITH REFRACTION.

Refraction in Action

Put the pencil or the pen into the glass. Let it lean against the side of the glass. Hold the glass so the top of the water is level with your eyes. Look at the pencil. It appears to be bent! Why?

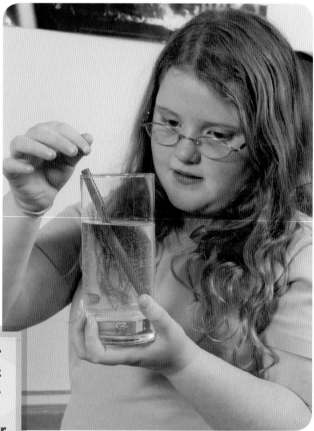

This pen looks bent or broken when part of it is put into water. The part of the pen in the water also looks thicker.

The top of the pencil is in the air. Light rays reflected from this part of the pencil travel quickly. Light rays reflected from the bottom of the pencil travel through the water. Light rays travel more slowly in water than in air. When the light rays leave the water, they speed up.

REFRACTION

pencil

glass

water

Light rays slow down and bend when they enter water.

The rays bouncing off the bottom of the pencil are refracted as they speed up. The rays change direction and make the pencil seem bent. But if you pull the pencil out of the glass, you can see that it isn't bent.

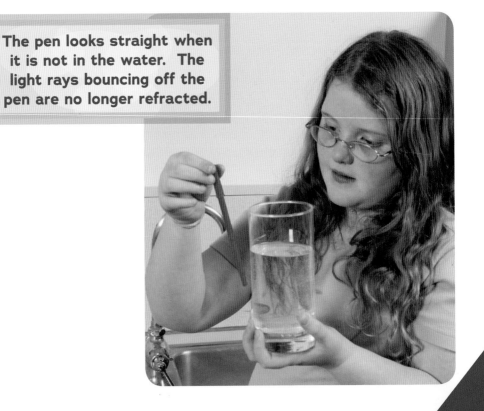

The pen looks straight when it is not in the water. The light rays bouncing off the pen are no longer refracted.

Chapter 5

COLORS

Sunlight is called white light. But white light contains many different colors mixed together. It has all the colors in the rainbow! A simple experiment will help you prove this.

Light might look white. But it is really made up of many colors. What kind of light is made up of every color?

Testing It Out

You will need a shallow baking pan, water, a mirror, and a flashlight.

Fill the pan with water. Place it on a table or a counter near a wall. Lean the mirror against the edge of the pan farthest from the wall. Half of the mirror should be out of the water.

You might need to use some tape or put a weight in front of the mirror to hold it up.

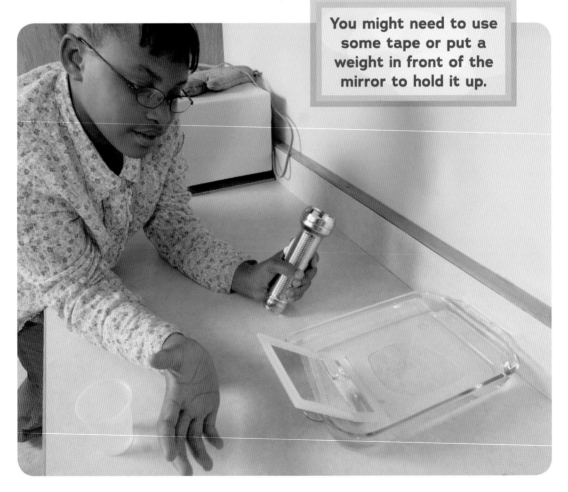

Shine the flashlight at the part of the mirror that is under the water. A rainbow will appear on the wall. You have split white light from the flashlight into many colors. What makes the colors appear?

Try lowering the mirror or moving the flashlight beam to get the rainbow to appear.

Refraction makes the colors appear. Light acts like a wave. A wave is like a line that keeps moving up and down. The distance from one top point to the next top point is the wavelength.

Each color of light has a different wavelength. Blue light has a short wavelength. Red light has the longest wavelength. Each color of wave is refracted a different amount.

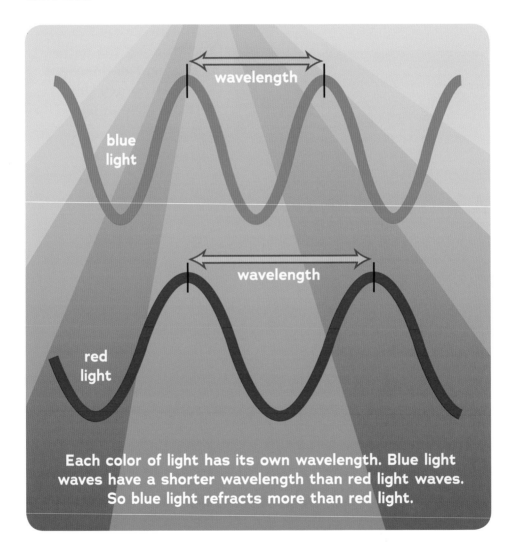

Each color of light has its own wavelength. Blue light waves have a shorter wavelength than red light waves. So blue light refracts more than red light.

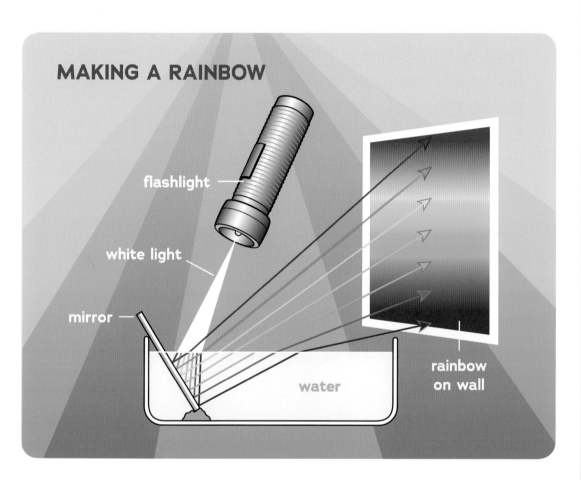

MAKING A RAINBOW

flashlight

white light

mirror

water

rainbow
on wall

When white light travels into the water, all the light waves are refracted. Each wavelength of light bends different amounts. This separates the white light into colors. Then the mirror reflects the waves to the wall. Our eyes see them as separate colors. We can see all the colors at once. We see a rainbow.

Objects Have Different Colors

Each object absorbs and reflects light waves differently. Because of this, objects have different colors. When an object reflects all light waves, it looks white.

When you see a red apple, you are seeing red light waves. The apple reflects red light waves. Light waves of other colors are absorbed into the apple.

You see a red apple because all the colors except red are absorbed into the apple. Red light is reflected from the apple's skin.

Chapter 6

LIGHT AND HEAT

When an object absorbs all colors of light, it looks black. What happens to matter when light waves are absorbed? When light rays are absorbed, they make matter get hot.

When you are outside on a sunny day, you will feel warmer wearing a black shirt than wearing a white one. Do you know why?

Experiment Time Again!

You can prove this with four sheets of paper, two white and two black. You'll also need tape, a scissors, a thermometer, water, and two identical glasses.

> **For this experiment, use two glasses that are the same. If the glasses are different, the experiment won't work as well.**

Fill both glasses with cool water. Take the temperature of the water in each glass. Write down the temperatures. The water in both glasses should be about the same temperature.

Wrap one glass with white paper. Cover the top of the glass with a small piece of white paper. Do the same thing to the other glass using the black paper.

Put the glasses next to each other in direct sunlight. Wait thirty minutes. Take the temperature of the water in each glass. Have the temperatures changed?

Do this experiment in the middle of the day. The sun's rays shine brightest then.

Absorbing and Refracting Rays

The water in the glass covered with black paper is much warmer. Why? The black paper has absorbed all the light rays. The absorbed rays heated the water.

The water in the glass covered with white paper hasn't heated up as much. Why? The white paper reflected most of the light rays. Fewer rays were absorbed. So the water didn't get as warm as the water in the other glass.

The white paper reflected most of the light rays.

You have learned a lot about light. Sunlight warms Earth. Light brightens a dark place. It adds color to your life. The next time you look in a mirror, think of light. Without it, your reflection wouldn't be there!

You can see yourself in a mirror because of light. It is reflecting off the mirror to your eyes.

Glossary

absorb: to soak up or take in

atom: a very tiny particle that makes up all things

energy: the ability to do work

matter: anything that can be weighed and takes up space. Matter can be a solid, a liquid, or a gas.

molecule: a group of atoms that are joined together

opaque: blocking light rays completely

photon: a tiny packet of light energy

ray: a narrow beam of light

reflect: to bounce off matter

refraction: the bending of light as it passes from one material to another

translucent: letting some light pass through, but not all

transparent: lets all light pass through so that objects on the other side can be seen clearly

wavelength: the distance on a wave from one top point to the next top point

Learn More about Light

Books

Ballard, Carol. *Exploring Light*. New York: PowerKids Press, 2008. This book explains where light comes from, how light travels, and how we see.

Cook, Trevor. *Experiments with Light and Sound*. New York: PowerKids Press, 2009. Hands-on experiments teach all about light and sound.

Stille, Darlene R. *Light*. Chanhassen, MN: Child's World, 2005. Learn about how light moves, the colors of light, and how we use light.

Walker, Sally M. *Investigating Electricity*. Minneapolis: Lerner Publications Company, 2012. Explore electricity and its connection to light in this informative book.

Websites

BBC Bitesize Science: Light and Shadows
http://www.bbc.co.uk/schools/ks2bitesize/science/physical_processes/light_shadows/play.shtml
This website features fun games related to light and shadows.

Dragonfly TV: Light and Color
http://pbskids.org/dragonflytv/show/lightandcolor.html
Watch a movie showing how five students used light and color to complete a project for their school's science club, and read about how you can experiment with light and color.

The NASA SCI Files: Light and Color
http://scifiles.larc.nasa.gov/text/kids/Problem_Board/problems/light/sim1.html
This useful site explains how and why we see different colors.

Index

Photo Acknowledgments

All images provided by Andy King except for the following: © Rubberball/Mark Andersen/Getty Images, cover; © Feverpitched/Dreamstime.com, p. 32. Illustrations by © Laura Westlund/ Independent Picture Service.

Main body text set in Adrianna Regular 14/20.
Typeface provided by Chank.